POETRY FROM CRESCENT MOON

The Crescent Moon Book of Mystical Poetry in English
edited by Carol Appleby

The Crescent Moon Book of Nature Poetry From Langland to Lawrence
edited by Margaret Elvy

The Crescent Moon Book of Metaphysical Poetry
edited and introduced by Charlotte Greene

The Crescent Moon Book of Elizabethan Love Poetry
edited and introduced by Carol Appleby

The Crescent Moon Book of Romantic Poetry
edited and introduced by L.M. Poole

Blinded By Her Light The Love-Poetry of Robert Graves
by Jeremy Mark Robinson

Peter Redgrove: Here Comes the Flood
by Jeremy Mark Robinson

Sex-Magic-Poetry-Cornwall: A Flood of Poems
by Peter Redgrove, edited with an essay by Jeremy Mark Robinson

Brigitte's Blue Heart
by Jeremy Reed

Claudia Schiffer's Red Shoes
by Jeremy Reed

By-Blows: Uncollected Poems
by D.J. Enright

Petrarch, Dante and the Troubadours: The Religion of Love and Poetry
by Cassidy Hughes

Dante: *Selections From the Vita Nuova*
translated by Thomas Okey

Arthur Rimbaud: *Selected Poems*
edited and translated by Andrew Jary

Arthur Rimbaud: *A Season in Hell*
edited and translated by Andrew Jary

Rimbaud: Arthur Rimbaud and the Magic of Poetry
by Jeremy Mark Robinson

Friedrich Hölderlin: *Hölderlin's Songs of Light: Selected Poems*
translated by Michael Hamburger

Heavenly Love:
Selected Poems

Heavenly Love:
Selected Poems

Edmund Spenser

Edited by Teresa Page

CRESCENT MOON

CRESCENT MOON PUBLISHING
P.O. Box 1312, Maidstone
Kent, ME14 5XU
Great Britain, www.crmoon.com

First published 1994. Second edition 2008. Revised 2014 and 2016.
Introduction © Teresa Page, 1994, 2008, 2014, 2016.

Printed and bound in the U.S.A.
Set in Garamond Book 10 on 12pt.
Designed by Radiance Graphics.

The right of Teresa Page to be identified as the editor of *Heavenly Love: Selected Poems* has been asserted generally in accordance with sections 77 and 78 of the Copyright, Designs and Patents Act 1988.

British Library Cataloguing in Publication data
Spenser, Edmund
Poems. - (British Poets Series)
I. Title II. Page, Teresa
III. Series
821.3

ISBN-13 9781861711427
ISBN-13 9781861715333

CONTENTS

from THE FAERIE QUEEN

Book Four, Canto X

Scudamour doth his conquest tell,
Of vertuous Amoret:
Great Venus temple is describ'd,
And lovers life forth set.

1

True he it said, what ever man it said,
That love with gall and hony doth abound,
But if the one be with the other wayd,
For every dram of hony therein found,
A pound of gall doth over it redound.
That I too true by triall have approved:
For since the day that first with deadly wound
My heart was launcht, and learned to have loved,
I never joyed howre, but still with care was moved.

2

And yet such grace is given them from above,
That all the cares and evil which they meet,
All their settled mindes remove,
But seeme gainst common sence to them most sweet;
As boosting in their martyrdome unmeet.
So all that ever yet I have endured,
I count as naught, and tread downe under feet,
Since of my love at length I rest assured,
That to disloyalty she will not be allured.

3

Long were to tell the travell and long toile,
Through which this shield of love I late have wonne,
And purchased this peerelesse beauties spoile,
That harder may be ended, then begonne.
But since ye so desire, your will be donne.
Then hearke ye gentle knights and Ladies free,
my hard mishaps, that ye may learne to shonne;
For though sweet love to conquer glorious bee,
Yet is the paine thereof much greater then the fee.

4

What time the fame of this renowned prise
Flew first abroad, and all mens eares possesst,
I having armes then taken, gan avise
To winne me honour by some noble gest,
And purchase me some place amongst the best.
I boldly thought (so young mens thoughts are bold)
That this same brave emprize for me did rest,
And that both shield and she whom I behold,
Might be my lucky lot; sith all by lot we hold.

5

So on that hard adventure forth I went,
And to the place of perill shortly came.
That was a temple faire and auncient,
Which of great mother Venus bare the name,
And farre renowmed through exceeeding fame;
Much more then that, which was in Paphos built,
Or that in Cyprus, both long since this same,
Though all the pillours of the one were guilt,
And all the others pavement were with ivory spilt.

6

And it was seated in an Island strong,
Abounding all with delices most rare,
And wall'd by nature gainst invaders wrong,
That none mote have accesse, nor inward fare,

But by one way, that passage did prepare.
It was a bridge ybuilt in goodly wize,
With curious Corbes and pendants graven faire,
And arched all with porches, did arize
On stately pillours, fram'd after the Doricke guize.

7

And for defence thereof, on th' other end
There reared was a castle faire and strong,
That warded all which in oor ut did wend,
And flancked both the bridges sides along,
Gainst all that would it faine to force or wrong.
And therein wonned twenty valiant knights;
All twenty tride in warres experience long;
Whose office as, against all manner wights
By all meanes to maintaine that castels ancient rights.

8

Before that Castle was an open plaine,
And in the midst thereof a piller placed;
On which this shield, of many sought in vaine,
The shield of Love, whose guerdon me hath graced,
Was hangd on high with golden ribbands laced;
And in the marble stone was written this,
With golden letters goodly well enchaced,
Blessed the man that well can use his blis:
Whose ever be the shield, faire Amoret be his.

9

Which when I red, my heart did inly earne,
And pant with hope of that adventures hap:
Ne stayed further newes thereof to learne,
But with my speare upon the shield did rap,
That all the castle ringed with the clap.
Streight forth issewd a Knight all arm'd to proofe,
And bravely mounted to his most mishap
Who staying nought to question from aloofe,
Ran fierce at me, that fire glaunst from his horses hoofe.

13

10

Whom boldly I encountered (as I could)
And by good fortune shortly him unseated.
Eftsoones out sprung two more of equall mould;
But I them both with equall hap defeated:
So all the twenty I likewise entreated,
And left them groning there upon the plaine.
Then preacing to the pillour I repeated
The read thereof for guerdon of my paine,
And taking downe the shield, with me did it retaine.

11

So forth without impediment I past,
Till to the Bridges utter gate I came:
The which I found sure lockt and chained fast.
I knockt, but no man aunswerd to my clame.
Yet I persever'd still; to knocke and call,
Till at the last I spide within the same,
Whereone stood peeping through a creuissmall,
To whom I cald aloud, halfe angry therewithal.

12

That was to weet the Porter of the place,
Unto whose trust the charge thereof was lent:
His name was Doubt, that had a double face,
Th' one forward looking, th' other backeward bent,
Therein resembling Ianus auncient,
Which hath in charge the ingate of the yeare:
And evermore his eyes about him went,
As if some proved perill he did feare,
Or did misdoubt some ill, whose cause did not appeare.

13

On th' one side he, on th' other sate Delay,
Behinde the gate, that none her might espy
Whose manner was all pasengers to stay,
And entertaine with her occassions sly,

Through which some lost great hope unheedily,
Which never they recover might againe;
And others quite excluded forth, did ly
Long languishing there in unpitted paine,
And seeking often entraunce, afterwards in vaine.

14

Me when as he had privily espide,
Bearing the shield which I had conquerd late,
He kend it streight, and to me opened wide.
So in I past, and streight he closd the gate
But being in, Delay in close awaite
Caught hold on me, and thought my steps to stay,
Feigning full many a fond excuse to prate,
And time to steale, the threasure of mans day,
Whose smellest minute lost no riches render may.

15

But no meanes my way I would forslow,
For ought that ever she could doe or say,
But from my lofty steede dismounting low,
Past forth on foote, beholding all the way
The goodly workes, and stones of rich assay,
Cast into sundry shapes by wondrous skill,
That like on earth no where I recken may:
And underneath, the river rolling still
With murmure soft, that seem'd to serve the workmans will.

16

Thence forth I passed to the second gate,
The Gate of good desert, whose goodly pride
And costly frame, were long here to relate.
The same to all stoode always open wide:
But in the Porch did evermore abide
An hideous Giant, dreadfull to behold,
That stopt the entraunce with his spacious stride,
And with the terrour of his countenance bold
Full many did affray, that else faine enter would.

17

His name was Daunger dreaded over all,
Who day and night did watch and duely ward,
From fearefull cowards, entrance to forstall,
And faint-heart-fooles, whom shew of perill hard
Could terrifie from Fortunes faire adward:
For oftentimes faint hearts at first espiall
Of his grim face, were from approaching scard;
Unworthy they of grace, whom one deniall
Excludes from fairest hope, withouten further triall.

18

Yet many doughty warriours, often ride
In greater perils to be stout and bold,
Durst not the sternnesse of his looke abide,
But soone as they his countenance did behold,
Began to faint, and feele their corage cold.
Againe some other, that in hard assayes
Were cowards knowne, and litle count did hold,
Either through gifts, or guile, or such like wayes,
Crept in by stouping low, or stealing of the kayes.

19

But I though meanest man of many moe,
Yet much disdaining unto him to lout,
Or creepe betweene his legs, so in to goe,
Resolv'd him to assault with manhood stout,
And either beat him in, or drive him out.
Eftsoones advancing that enchaunted shield,
With al my might I gan to lay about:
Which when he saw, the glaiue which he did wield
He gan forthwith t' avale, and way unto me yield.

20

So as I entred, I did backeward looke,
For feare of harme, that might lie hidden there;
And loe his hindparts, whereof heed I tooke,

Much more deformed fearefull ugly were,
Then all his former parts did earst appere.
For hatred, murther, treason, and despright,
With many moe lay in ambushment there,
Awayting to entrap the warelesse wight,
Which did not them prevent with vigilant foresight.

21

Thus having past all perill, I was come
Within the compasse of that Islands space;
The which did seeme unto my simple doome
The onely pleasant and delightfull place,
That ever troden was of footings trace.
For all that nature by her mother wit
Could frame in earth, and former of substance base,
Was there, and all that nature did omit,
Art playing second natures part, supplied it.

22

No tree, that is of count, in greenewood growes,
From lowest Juniper to Ceder tall,
No flowre in field, that daintie odour throwes,
And deckes his branch with blossomes over all,
But there was planted, or grew naturall:
Nor sense of man so coy and curious nice,
But there mote find to please it selfe withall;
Nor hart could wish for any queint device,
But there it present was, and did fraile sense entice.

23

In such luxurious plentie of all pleasure,
It seem'd a second paradise to ghesse,
So lavishly enricht with natures treasure,
That if the happie soules, which doe possesse
Th' Elysian fields, and live in lasting blesse,
Should happen this with living eye to see,
They soone would loath their lesser happinesse,
And wish to life return'd againe to bee,

That in this joyous place they mote have joyance free.

24

Fresh shadowes, fit to shroud from sunny ray;
Faire lawnds, to take the sunne in season dew;
Sweet springs, in which a thousand nymphs did play;
Soft rombling brookes, that gentle slomber drew;
High reared mounts, the lands about to view;
Low looking dales, disloigned from common gaze;
Delightfull bowres, to solace lovers trew;
False Labyrinthes, fond runners eyes to daze;
All which by nature made did nature selfe amaze.

25

And all without were walkes and alleyes dight
With divers trees, enrang'd in even rankes;
And here and there were pleasant arbors pight.
And shadie seates, and sundry flowring bankes,
To sit and rest the walkers wearie shankes,
And therein thousand payres of lovers walkt,
Praysing their god, and yeelding him great thankes,
Ne ever ought but of their true loves talkt,
Ne ever for rebuke or blame of any balkt.

26

All these together by themselves did sport
Their spotlesse pleasures, and sweet loves content.
But farre away from these, another sort
Of lovers lincked in true harts consent;
Which loved not as these, for like desire,
Farre from all fraud, or fayned blandishment;
Which in their spirits kindling zealous fire,
Brave thoughts and noble deedes did evermore aspire.

27

Such were great Hercules, and Hylas deare;
Trew Jonanthan, and David trustie tryde;
Stout Theseus, and Pirithous his feare;
Pylades and Orestes by his side;
Mild Titus and Gesippus without pride;
Damon and Pythias whom death could not sever:
All these and all that ever had bene tide
In bands of friendship, there did live for ever,
Whose lives although decay'd, yet loves decayed never.

28

Which when as I, that never tasted blis,
Nor happie howre, beheld with gazefull eye,
I thought there was none other heaven then this;
And gan their endlesse happinesse enuye,
That being free from feare and gealoyse,
Might frankely there their loves desire possesse;
Whilest I through paines and perlous jeopardie,
Was forst to seeke my lifes deare patronesse:
Much dearer be the things, which come through hard distresse.

29

Yet all those sights, and all that else I saw,
Might not my steps withhold, but that forthright
Unto that purposd place I did me draw,
Where as my love was lodged day and night:
The temple of great Venus, that is hight
The Queene of beautie, and of love the mother,
There worshipped of every living wight;
Whose goodly workmanship farre past all other
That ever were on earth, all were they set together.

30

Not that same famous Temple of Diane,
Whose high all Ephesus did oversee,
And which all Asia sought with vowes prophane,

One of the worlds seven wonders sayd to bee,
Might match with this by many a degree:
Nor that, which that wise King of Jurie framed,
With endlesse cost, to be th' Almighties see;
Nor all that else through all the world is named
To all the heathen Gods, might like to this be clamed.

31

I much admyring that so goodly frame,
Unto the porch approcht, which open stood;
But therein sate an amiable Dame,
That seem'd to be of very sober mood,
And in her semblant shewed great womanhood:
Strange was her tyre; for on her head a crowne
She wore much like unto a Danisk hood,
Poudred with pearle and stone, and all her gowne
Enwoven was with gold, that raught full low a downe.

32

On either side of her, two young men stood,
Both strongly arm'd, as fearing one another;
Yet were they brethren both of halfe the blood,
Begotten by two fathers of one mother,
Though of contrarie natures each to other:
The one of them high Love, the other hate,
Hate was the elder, Love the younger brother;
Yet was the younger stronger in his state
Then th' elder, and him maystred still in all debate.

33

Nathlesse that Dame so well them tempred both,
That she them forced hand to joyne in hand,
Albe that Hatred was thereto full loth,
And turn'd his face away, as he did stand,
Unwilling to behold that lovely band.
Yet she was of such grace and vertuous might,
That her commaundment he could not withstand,
But by his lip for felonous despright,

And gnasht his iron tuskes at that displeasing sight.

34

Concord she cleeped was in common reed,
Mother of blessed Peace, and Friendship trew;
They both her twins, both borne of heavenly seed,
And she her selfe likewise divinely grew;
The which right well her workes divine did shew:
For strength, and wealth, and happinese she lends,
And strife, and warre, and anger does subdew:
Of little much, of foes she maketh frends,
And to afflicted minds sweet rest and quiet sends.

35

By her the heaven is in his course contained,
And all the world in state unmoved stands,
As their Almightie maker first ordained,
And bound them with inviolable bands;
Else would the waters overflow the lands,
And fire devoure the aire, and hell them quight,
But that she holds them with her blessed hands.
She is the nourse of pleasure and delight,
And unto Venus grace the gate doth open right.

36

By her I entring halfe dismayed was,
But she in gentle wise me entertayned,
And twixt her selfe and Love did let me pass;
But Hatred would my entrance have restrayned,
And with his club me threatned to have betrayned,
Had not the Ladie with her powreful speach
Him from his wicked will uneath refrayned;
And th' other eke his malice did empeach,
Till I was throughly past the perill of his reach.

37

Into the inmost Temple thus I came,
Which fuming all with frankensence I found,
And odours rising from the altars flame.
Upon an hundred marble pillors round
The roofe up high as reared from the ground,
All deckt with crownes, and chaynes, and girlands gay,
And thousand pretious gifts worth many a pound,
The which sad lovers for their vows did pay;
And all the ground was strow'd with flowres, as fresh as May.

38

An hundred Altars round about were set,
All flaming with their sacrifices fire,
That with the steme thereof the Temple swet,
Which rould in clouds to heaven did aspire,
And in them bore true lovers vowes entire:
And eke an hundred brasen cauldrons bright,
To bath in joy and amorous desire,
Every of which was to a damzell hight;
For all the Priests were damzels, in soft linnen dight.

39

Right in the midst the Goddess selfe did stand
Upon an altar of some costly masse,
Whose substance was uneath to understand:
For neither pretious stone, nor durefull brasse,
Nor shining gold, nor mouldring clay it was;
But much more rare and pretious to esteeme,
Pure in aspect, and like to christall glasse,
Yet glasse was not, if one did rightly deeme,
But being faire and brickle, likest glasse did seeme.

40

But it in shape and beautie did excel
All other Idoles, which the heathen adore,
Farre passing that, which by surpassing skill

Phidias did make in Paphos Isle of yore,
With which that wretched Greeke, that life forlore,
Did fall in love: yet this much faire shined,
But covered with a slender veile afore;
And both her feete and legs together twined
Were with a snake, whose head and tail were fast combined.

41

The cause why she was covered with a vele,
Was hard to know, for that her Priests the same
From peoples knowledge labour'd to concele.
But sooth it was not sure for womanish shame,
Nor any blemish, which the worke mote blame;
But for, they say, she hath both kinds in one,
Both male and female, both under one name:
She syre and mother is her selfe alone,
Begets and eke conceives, ne needeth other none.

42

And all about her necke and shoulders flew
A flocke of litle loves, and sports, and joyes,
With nimble wings of gold and purple hew;
Whose shapes seem'd not like to terrestriall boyes,
But like to Angels playing heavenly toyes;
The whilst their eldest brother was away,
Cupid their eldest brother; he enjoyes
The wide kingdome of love with Lordly sway,
And to his law compels all creatures to obay.

43

And all about her altar scattered lay
Great sorts of lovers piteously complayning,
Some of their losse, some of their loves delay,
Some of their pride, some paragons disdayning,
Some feare fraud, some fraudulently fayning,
As every one had cause of good or ill.
Amongst the rest someone through lovers constrayning,
Tormented sore, could not containe it still.

But thus brake forth, that all the temple it did fill.

44

Great Venus, Queene of beautie and of grace,
The joy of Gods and men, that under skie
Doest fayrest shine, and most adorne thy place,
That with thy smiling looke doest pacifie
The raging seas, and makst the stormes to flie;
Thee goddesse, thee the winds, the clouds does feare,
And when thou spredst thy mantle forth on hie,
The waters play and pleasant lands appeare,
And heavens laugh, and all the world shews joyous cheare.

45

Then doth the daedale earth throw forth to thee
Out of her fruitfull lap aboundant flowres,
And then all living weights, soone as they see
The spring breake forth out of his lusty bowres,
They all doe learne to play the Paramours;
First doe the merry birds, thy pretty pages
Primly pricked with thy lustfull powres,
Chirpe loud to thee out of their leavy cages,
And thee their mother call to coole their kindly rages.

46

Then doe the saluage beasts begin to play
Their pleasant friskes, and loath their wonted food;
The Lyons rore, the Tygres loudly bray,
The raging Bulls rebellow through the wood,
And breaking forth, dare tempt the deepest flood,
To come where thou doest draw them with desire:
So all things else, that nourish vitall blood,
Soone as with fury thou doest theminspire,
In generation seeke to quench their inward fire.

47

So all the world by thee at first was made,
And dayly yet thou doest the same repayre:
Ne ought on earth that merry is and glad,
No ought on earth that lovely is and fayre,
But thou the same for pleasure didst prepayre.
Thou art the root of all that joyous is,
Great God of men and women, queene of th' ayre,
Mother of laughter, and welspring of blisse,
O graunt that of my love at last I may not misse.

48

So did he say: but I with murmure soft,
That none might heare the sorrow of my hart,
Yet inly groning deepe and sighing oft,
Besought her to graunt ease unto my smart,
And to my wound her gratious help impart.
Whilest thus I spake, behold with happy eye
I spyde, where at the idoles feet apart
A bevie of fayre damzels close did lie,
Waiting when as the Antheme should be sung in hie.

49

The first of them did seeme of riper yeares,
And graver countenance then all the rest;
Yet all the rest were eke her equall peares,
Yet unto her obayed all the best.
Her name was Womanhood, that she exprest
By her sad semblant and demeanure wise:
For stedfast still her eyes did fixed rest,
Ne rov'd at random after gauzes guyse,
Whose luring baites oftimes doe heedlesse harts entyse.

50

And next to her sate goodly Shamefastnesse,
Ne ever durst her eyes from ground upreare,
Ne ever once did looke up from her desse,

As if some blame of evill she did feare,
That in her cheekes made roses oft appeare.
And her against sweet Cherefulnesse was placed,
Whose eyes like twinkling stars in evening cleare,
Were deckt with smiles, that all sad humors chaced,
And darted forth delights, the which her goodly graced.

51

And next to her sate sober Modestie,
Holding her hand upon her gentle hart;
And her against sate comely Curtesie,
That unto every person knew her part;
And her before was seated overthwart
Soft Silence, and submisse Obedience,
Both linckt together never to dispart,
Both gifts of God not gotten but from thence,
Both girlonds of his Saints against their foes offence.

52

Thus sate they all a round in seemely rate:
And in the midst of them a goodly maid,
Even in the lap of Womanhood there sate,
The which was all in lilly white arayed,
With silver streames amongst the linnen stray'd;
Like to the Morne, when first her syning face
Hath to the gloomy world it selfe bewray'd,
That same was fairest Amoret in place,
Shining with beauties light, and heavenly vertues grace.

53

Whom soone as I beheld, my hart gan throb,
And wade in doubt, what best were to be donne:
For sacrilege me seem'd the church to rob,
And folly seem'd to leave the thing undonne,
Which with so strong atempt I had begonne.
Tho shaking off all doubt and shamefast feare,
Which Ladies love I heard had never wonne
Mongst men of worth, I to her stepped neare,

And by the lilly hand her labour'd up to reare.

54

Thereat that formost matrone me did blame,
And sharpe rebuke, for being over bold;
Saying it was to Knight unseemly shame,
Upon a recluse Virgin to lay hold,
That unto Venus services was sold.
To whom I thus, Nay but it fitteth best,
For Cupids man with Venus maid to hold,
For ill your goddesse services are drest
By virgins, and her sacrifices let to rest.

55

With that my shield I forth to her did show,
Which all that while I closely had conceld;
On which when Cupid with his killing bow
And cruell shafts emblazoned she beheld,
At sight thereof she was with terror queld,
And said no more: but I which all that while
The pledge of faith, her hand engaged held,
Like warie Hynd within the weedie soile,
For no intreatie would forgoe so glorious spoile.

56

And evermore upon the Goddesse face
Mine eye was fixt, for feare of her offence,
Whom when I saw with amiable grace
To laugh at me, and favour my pretence,
I was emboldned with more confidence,
And nought for nicenesse nor for envy sparing,
In presence of them all forth led her thence,
All looking on, and like astonisht staring,
Yet to lay hand on her, not one of all them daring.

57

She often prayd, and often me besought,
Sometime with tender teares to let her goe,
Sometime with witching smyles: but yet for nought,
That ever she to me could say or doe,
Could she her wished freedome fro me wooe;
But forth I led her through the Temple gate,
By which I hardly past with much adoe:
But that same Ladie which me friended late
In entrance, did me also friend in my retrate.

58

No lesse did Daunger threaten me with dread,
When as he saw me, maugre all his powre,
That glorious spoile of beautie with me lead,
Then Cerberus, when Orpheus did recoure
His Leman from the Stygian Princes boure.
But evermore my shield did me defend,
Against the storme of every dreadfull stoure:
Thus safely with my love I thence did wend.
So ended he his tale, where I this Canto end.

from AMORETTI

1

Happy ye leaves when as those lilly hands,
    which hold my life in their dead doing might,
    shall handle you and hold in loves soft bands,
    lyke captives trembling at the victors sight.
And happy lines, on which with starry light,
    those lamping eyes will deigne sometimes to look
    and reade the sorrowes of my dying spright,
    written with teares in harts close bleeding book.
And happy rymes bath'd in the sacred brooke,
    of Helicon whence she derived is,
    when ye behold that Angels blessed looke,
    my soules long lacked foode, my heavens blis.
Leaves, lines, and rymes, seeke her to please alone,
    whom if ye please, I care for other none.

3

The souverayne beauty which I doo admyre,
 witnesse the world how worthy to be prayzed:
 the light wherof hath kindled heavenly fyre,
 in my fraile spirit by her from basenesse raysed.
That being now with her huge brightnesse dazed,
 base thing I can no more endure to view:
 but looking still on her I stand amazed,
 at wondrous sight of so celestiall hew.
So when my toung would speak her praises dew,
 it stopped is with thoughts astonishment:
 and when my pen would write her titles true,
 it ravisht is with fancies wonderment:
Yet in my hart I then both speake and write
 the wonder that my wit cannot endite.

8

More then most faire, full of the living fire,
>
>> kindled above unto the maker neere:
>> no eyes but joyes, in which all powers conspire,
>> that to the world naught else be counted deare.
>
Thrugh your bright beames doth not the blinded guest,
>
>> shoot out his darts to base affections wound:
>> but angels come to lead fraile mindes to rest
>> in chaste desires on heavenly beauty bound.
>
You frame my thoughts and fashion my within,
>
>> you stop my toung, and teach my hart to speake,
>> you calme the torme that passion did begin,
>> strong thrugh your cause, but by your vertue weak.
>
Dark is the world, where your light shined never;
>
>> well is he borne, that may behold you ever.

17

The glorious pourtraict of that Angels face,
      made to amaze weake mens confused skil:
      and this worlds worthlesse glory to embase,
      what pen, what pencil can expresse her fill?
For though he colours could devize at will,
      and eke his learned hand at pleasure guide,
      least trembling it his workmanship should spill,
      yet many wondrous things there are beside.
The sweet eye-glaunces, that like arrowes glide,
      the charming smiles, that rob sence from the hart:
      the lovely pleasance and the lofty pride,
      cannot expressed be by any art.
A greater craftesmans hand thereto doth neede,
      that can expresse the life of things indeed.

22

This holy season fit to fast and pray,
      men to devotion ought to be inclynd:
      therefore, I lykewise on so holy day,
      for my sweet Saynt some service fit will find.
Her temple fayre is built within my mind,
      in which her glorious image placed is,
      on which my thoughts do day and night attend
      lyke sacred priests that never thinke amisse.
There I to her as th'author of my blise,
      will builde an altar to appease her ire:
      and on the same my hart will sacrifise,
      burning in flames of pure and chast desyre:
The which vouchsafe O goddesse to accept,
      amongst thy deerest relicks to be kept.

34

Lyke as a ship that through the Ocean wide,
      by conduct of some star doth make her way,
      when as a storme hath dimd her trusty guide,
      out of her course doth wander far astray.
So I whose star, that wont with her bright ray,
      me to direct, with cloudes is overcast,
      doe wander now in darknesse and dismay,
      through hidden perils round about me plast.
Yet hope I well, that when this storme is past
      my Helice the lodestar of my life
      will shine again, and looke on me at last,
      with lovely light to cleare my cloudy grief.
Till then I wander carefull comfortlesse,
      in secret sorrow and sad pensivenesse.

38

Arion, when through tempests cruel wracke,
>he forth was thrown into the greedy seas:
>through the sweet musick which he harp did make
>allu'rd a Dolphin him from death to ease.
But my rude musick, which was wont to please
>some dainty eares, cannot with any skill,
>the dreadfull tempest of her wrath appease,
>nor move the Dolphin from her stubborne will.
But in her pride she dooth persever still,
>all carelesse how my life for her decayse:
>yet with one word she can it save or spill,
>to spill were pitty, but so save were prayse.
Chose rather to be praysd for dooing good,
>then to be blam'd for spilling guiltlesse blood.

39

Sweet smile, the daughter of the Queene of love,
    expresing all thy mothers powrefull art:
    with which she wonts to temper angry love,
    when all the gods he threats with thundring dart.
Sweet is thy vertue as thyselfe sweet art,
    for when on me thou shinedst late in sadnesse,
    a melting pleasance ran through every part,
    and me revived with hart robbing gladnesse.
Whylest rapt with joy resembling heavenly madnes,
    my soule was ravisht quite as in a traunce:
    and feeling thence no more her sorowes sadnesse,
    fed on the fulnesse of that chearefull glaunce,
More sweet than Nectar or Ambrosiall meat,
    seemd every bit, which thenceforth I did eat.

61

The glorious image of the makers beautie,
     my soverayne saynt, the Idoll of my thought,
     dare not henceforth above the bounds of dewtie,
     t'accuse of pride, or rashly blame for ought.
For being as she is divinely wrought,
     and of the brood of Angels heavenly borne:
     and with the crew of blessed Saynts upbrought,
     each of which did her with their guilts adorne;
The bud of joy, the blossome of the morne,
     the beame of light, whom mortal eyes admyre:
     what reason is it then but she should scorne
     base things, that to her love too bold aspire?
Such heavenly formes ought rather worshipt be,
     then dare be lov'd by men of meane degree.

64

Comming to kisse her lips, (such grace I found)
    me seemd I smelt a gardin of sweet flowers:
    that dainty odours from them threw around
    for damzels fit to decke their lovers bowres.
Her lips did smell like unto Gillyflowers,
    her ruddy cheekes like unto Roses red:
    her snowy browes like budded Bellamoures,
    her lovely eyes like Pincks but newly spred.
Her goodly bosome like a Strawberry bed,
    her neck like to a bounch of Cullambines:
    her brest like lillies, ere their leaves be shed,
    her nipples like young blossomd Jessemines.
Such fragrant flowres doe give most odorous smell,
    but her sweet odour did them all excell.

68

Most glorious Lord of life, that on this day,
   didst make thy triumph over death and sin:
   and having harrowd hell, didst bring away
   captivity thence captive us to win:
This joyous day, deare Lord, with joy begin,
   and grant that we for whom thou diddest die
   being with thy deare blood clene washt from sin,
   may live for ever in felicity.
And that thy love we weighing worthily,
   may likewise love thee for the same againe:
   and for thy sake that all like deare didst buy,
   with love may one another entertain.
So let us love, deare love, like as we ought,
   love is the lesson which the Lord we taught.

72

Oft when my spirit doth spred her bolder winges,
      in mind to mount up to the purest sky:
      it down is weighed with thought of earthly things
      and clogd with burden of mortality,
Where when that soverayne beauty it doth spy,
      resembling heavens glory in her light:
      drawne with sweet pleasure bait, it back doth fly,
      and unto heaven forgets her former flight.
There my fraile fancy fed with full delight,
      doth bath in blisse and mantleth most at ease:
      ne thinks of other heaven, but how it might
      her harts desire with most contentment please.
Hart need not with none other happinesse,
      but here on earth to have such heavens blisse.

76

Faire bosome fraught with vertues richest tresure,
  the neast of love, the lodging of delight:
  the bowre of blisse, the paradice of pleasure,
  the sacred harbour of that heavenly spright.
How was I ravisht with your lovely sight,
  and my fraile thoughts too rashly led astray?
  whiles diving deepe through amorous insight,
  on the sweet spoile of beautie they did pray.
And twixt her paps like early fruit in May.
  whose harvest seemd to hasten now apace:
  they loosely did their wanton winges display,
  and there to rest themselves did boldly place.
Sweet thoughts I envy your so happy rest,
  which oft I wisht, yet never as so blest.

82

Joy of my life, full oft for loving you
    I blesse my lot, that was so lucky placed:
    but then the more your owne mishap I rew,
    that are so much by so meane love embased.
For had the equall heavens so much you graced
    in this as in the rest, ye mote invent
    some heavenly wit, whose verse could have enchased
    your glorious name in golden moniment.
But since ye deignd so goodly to relent
    to me your thrall, in whom is little worth,
    that little that I am, shall all be spent,
    in setting your immortall prayses forth.
Whose lofty argument uplifting me,
    shall lift you up unto an high degree.

from

EPITHALAMION

Bring with you all the Nymphes that you can heare
Both of the rivers and the forrests greene:
And of the sea that neighbours to her neare,
All with gay girlands goodly wel beseene.
And let them also with them bring in hand,
Another gay girland
For my faire love of lillies and of roses,
Bound truelove wize with a blew silke riband.
And let them make great store of bridale poses,
And let them eeke bring store of other flowers
To deck the bridale bowers.
And let the ground whereas her foot shall tread,
For feare the stones her tender foot should wrong
Be strewed with fragrant flowers all along,
And diapred like the discolored mead.
Which done, doe at her chamber dore awayt,
For she will waken strayt,
The whiles doe ye this song unto her sing,
The woods shall to you answer and your Eccho ring.

•

Wake, now my love, awake; for it is time,
The Rosy Morne long since left Tithones bed,
All ready to her silver coche to clyme,
And Phoebus gins to shew his glorious hed.
Hark how the cheerfull birds do chaunt their lays
And carroll of loves praise.
The merry Larke hir mattins sings aloft,
The thrush replies, the Mavis descant playes.
The ouzell shrills, the Ruddock warbles soft,
So goodly al agree with sweet consent,

To this dayes merriment.
Ah my deere love why doe ye sleepe thus long,
When meeter were that ye should now awake,
T'awayt the comming of your joyous make,
And hearken to the birds lovelearned song,
The deawy leaves among.
For they of joy and pleasance to you sing,
That all the woods them answer and their eccho ring.

•

Tel me ye merchants daughters did ye see
Se faire a creature in your towne before,
So sweet, so lovely, and so mild as she,
Adornd with beautyes grace and vertues store,
Her goodly eyes like Saphyres shining bright,
Her forehead ivory white,
Her cheekes like apples which the sun hath rudded,
Her lips like cherries charming men to bite,
Her brest like to a bowle of creame uncrudded,
Her paps like lillies budded,
Her snowie necke like to a marble towre,
And all her body like a pallace faire,
Ascending uppe with many a stately staire,
To honors seat and chastities sweet bowre.
Why stand ye still ye virgins in amaze,
Upon her so to gaze,
Whiles ye forget your former lay to sing,
To which the woods did answer and your eccho ring.

•

Now ceasse ye damsels your delights forepast;
Enough is it, that all the day was youres:
Now day is done, and night is nighing fast:
Now bring the Bride into the bridall boures.
Now night is come, now sone her disaray,
And in her bed her lay;
Lay her in lillies and in violets,
And silken courteins over her display,
And odourd sheetes, and Arras coverlets.
Behold how goodly my faire love does ly
In proud humility;
Like unto Maia, when as love her tooke,

In Tempe, lying on the flowry gras,
Twixt sleepe and wake, after she weary was,
With bathing in the Acidalian brooke.
Now it is night, ye damsels may be gon,
And leave my love alone,
And leave likewise your former lay to sing:
The woods no more shal answere, nor your echo ring.

from A HYMN IN HONOUR OF LOVE

For love is Lord of truth and loyaltie,
Lifting himselfe out of the lowly dust,
On golden plumes up to the purest skie,
Above the reach of loathly sinfull lust,
Whose base affect through cowardly distrust
Of his weake wings, dare not to heaven fly,
But like a moldwarpe in the earth doth ly.

His dunghill thoughts, which do themselves enure
To dirtie drosse, no higher dare aspire,
Ne can his feeble earthly eyes endure
The flaming light of that celestiall desire,
And makes him mount above the native might
Of heavie earth, up to the heavens light.

Such is the powre of that sweet passion,
That it all sordid basenesse doth expell,
And the refined mind doth newly fashion
Unto a fairer forme, which now doth dwell
In his high thought, that would itselfe excell;
Which he beholding still with constant sight,
Admires the mirrour of so heavenly light.

Whose image printing in his deepest wit,
He thereon feeds his hungrie fantasy,
Still full, yet never satisfyde with it,
Like Tantale, that in store doth sterued ly:
So doth he pine in most satiety,
For nought may quench his infinite desire,
Once kindled through that first conceived fire.

from A HYMN IN HONOUR OF BEAUTY

For when the soule, the which derived was
At first, out of that great immortall Spright,
By whom all live to love, whilome did pas
Downe from the top of purest heavens hight,
To be embodied here, it then tooke light
And lively spirits from that fairest starre,
Which lights the world forth from his firie carre.

•

So every spirit, as it is most pure,
And hath in it the more of heavenly light,
So it the fairer bodie doth procure
To habit in, and it more fairely dight
With chearfull grace and amiable sight.
For of the soule the bodie forme doth take:
For soule is forme, and doth the bodie make.

•

But gentle Love, that loyall is and trew,
Will more illumine your resplendent ray,
And adde more brightnesse to your goodly hew,
From light of his pure fire, which by like way
Kindled of yours, your likenesse doth display,
Like as two mirrours by opposd reflexion,
Doe both expresse the faces first impression.

47

Therefore to make your beautie more appeare,
It you behoves to love, and forth to lay
That heavenly riches, which in you ye beare,
That men the more admire their fountaine may,
For else what booteth that celestiall ray,
If it in darknesse be enshrined ever,
That it of loving eyes be vewed never?

•

For Love is a celestiall harmonie,
Of likely harts composd of starres concent,
Which joine together in sweete sympathie,
To worke ech others joy and true content,
Which they have harbourd since their first descent
Out of their heavenly bowres, where they did see
And know ech other here belov'd to bee.

Then Io triumph, O great beauties Queene,
Advance the banner of thy conquest hie,
That all this world, the which thy vassals beene,
May draw to thee, and with dew fealtie,
Adore the powre of thy great Majestie,
Singing this Hymne in honour of thy name,
Compyld by me, which thy poore liegeman am.

In lieu whereof graunt, O great Soveraine,
That she whose conquering beautie doth captive
My trembling hart in her eternall chaine,
One drop of grace at length will to me give,
That I her bounden thrall by her may lieve,
And this same life, which first fro me she reaved,
May owe to her, of whom I it receaved.

And you faire Venus dearling, my deare dread,
Fresh flowre of grace, great Godesse of my life,
When your faire eyes these fearefull lines shal read,
Deigne to let fall one drop of dew reliefe,
That may recure my harts long pining griefe,
And shew what wondrous powre your beauty hath,
That can restore a damned virgin wight from death.

from A HYMN OF HEAVENLY LOVE

Love, lift me up upon thy golden wings,
From this base world unto thy heavens hight,
Where I maysee those admirable things,
Which there thou workest by thy soveraine might
Faire above feeble reach of earthly sight,
That I thereof an heavenly Hymn may sing
Unto the god of Love, high heavens king.

•

Yet o most blessed Spirit, pure lampe of light,
Eternalle spring of grace and wisedome trew,
Vouchsafe to shed into my barren spright,
Some little drop of thy celestiall dew,
That may my rymes with sweet infuse embrew,
And give me words equall unto my thought,
To tell the marveiles by thy mercie wrought.

Yet being pregnant still with powerfull grace,
And full of fruitfull love, that loves to get
Things like himselfe, and to enlarge his race,
His second brood though not in powre so great,
Yet full of beautie, next he did beget
An infinite increase of Angels bright,
All glistring glorious in their Makers light.

To them the heavens illimitable hight,
Not this round heaven, which we from hence behold,
Adornd with thousand lamps of burning light,
And with ten thousand gemmes of shining gold,
He gave as their inheritance to hold,
That they might serve him in eternall blis,
And be partakers of those joyes of his.

•

Then shalt thou feele thy spirit so possest,
And ravisht with devouring great desire
Of his deare selfe, that shall they feeble brest
Inflame with love, and set thee all on fire
With burning zeale, through every part entire,
That in no earthly thing thou shalt delight,
But in his sweet and amiable sight.

Thenceforth all worlds desire will in the dye,
And all earthes glorie on which men do gaze,
Seeme durt and drosse in thy pure sighted eye,
Compar'd to that celestiall beauties blaze,
Whose glorious beames all fleshly sense doth daze
With admiration of their passing light,
Blinding the eyes and lumining the spright.

Then shall thy ravisht soule inspired bee
With heavenly thoughts, farre above humane skill,
And thy bright radiant eyes shall plainely see
Th' Idee of his pure glorie, present still
Before thy face, that all thy spirits shall fill
With sweete enragement of celestial love,
Kindled through sight of those faire things above.

A HYMN OF HEAVENLY BEAUTY

Rapt with the rage of mine own ravisht thought,
Through contemplation of those goodly sights,
And glorious images in heaven wrought,
Whose wondrous beauty breathing sweet delights,
Do kindle love in high conceipted sprights:
I faine to tell the things that I behold,
But feede my wits to faile, and tongue to fold.

Vouchsafe then, O thou most almightie Spright,
From whom all guifts of wit and knowledge flow,
To shed into my breast some sparkling light
Of thine eternall Truth, that I may show
Some little beames to mortall eyes below,
Of that immortall beautie, there with thee,
Which in my weake distraughted mind I see.

That with the glorie of so goodly sight,
The hearts of men, which fondly here admire
Faire seeming shewes, and feed on vaine delight,
Transported with celestial desire
Of those faire formes, may lift themselves up hier,
And learne t olove with zealous humble dewty
Th' eternall fountaine of that heavenly beauty.

Beginning then below, with th'easie vew
Of this base world, subject to fleshly eye,
From thence to mount aloft by order dew,
To contemplation of th' immortall sky,
Of the soare faulcon so I learne to fly,

That flags awhile her fluttering wings beneath,
Till she her selfe for stronger flight can breath.

Then looke who list, thy gazefull eyes to feed
With sight of that is faire, looke on the frame
Of this wide universe, and therein reed
The endless kinds of creatures, which by name
Thou canst not count, much lesse their natures aime:
All which are made with wondrous wise respect,
And all with admirable beautie deckt.

First th' Earth, on adamantine pillers founded,
Amid the Sea engirt with brasen bands;
Then th' Aire still flitting, but yet firmely bounded,
On everie side, with piles of flaming brands,
Never consum'd nor quencht with mortall hands;
And last, that mightie shining christall wall,
Wherewith he hath encompassed this All.

By view whereof, it plainly may appeare,
That still as every thing doth upward tend,
And further is frome arth, so still more cleare
And faire it growes, till to his perfect end
Of purest beautie, it at last ascend:
Aire more then water, fire much more then aire,
And heaven then fire appeares more pure and faire.

Looke thou no further, but affixe thine eye
On that bright shinie round still moving masse,
The house of blessed Gods, which men call Skye,
Al sowd with glistring stars more thicke than grasse,
Whereof each other doth in brightnese passe;
But those two most, which ruling night and day,
As King and Queene, the heavens Empire sway.

And tell me then, what hast thou ever seene,
That to their beautie may compared bee,
Or can the sight that is most sharpe and keene,
Endure their Captains flaming head to see?
How much lesse those, much higher in degree,
And so much fairer, and much more then these,
As these are fairer then the land and seas?

For farre above these heavens which here we see,
Be others farre exceeding these in light,
Not bounded, not corrupt, as these same bee,
But infinite in largenesse and in hight,
Unmoving, uncorrupt, and spotlesse bright,
That need no Sunne t' illuminate their spheres,
But their owne native light farre passing theirs.

And as these heavens still by degrees arize,
Until they come to their first Movers bound,
That in his mightie compasse doth comprize,
And carries all the rest with him around,
So those likewise doe by degrees redound,
And rise more faire, till they at last arive
To the most faire, whereto they all do strive.

Faire is the heaven, where happy soules have place,
In full enjoyment of felicitie,
Whence they doe still behold the glorious face
Of the divine eternall Majestie;
More faire is that, where those Idees on hie,
Entraunged be, which Plato so admired,
And pure Intelligences from God inspired.

Yet fairer is that heaven, in which doe raine
The soveraine Powres and mightie Potentates,
Which in their high protections doe containe
All mortall Princes, and imperiall States;
And faire yet, whereas the royall Seates
And heavenly Dominations are set,
From whom all earthly goverance is fet.

Yet faire more faire be those bright Cherubins,
Which all with golden wings are overdight,
And those eternall burning Seraphins,
Which from their faces dart out fierie light;
Yet faire then they both, and much more bright
Be th' Angels and Archangels, which attend
On Gods owne person, without rest or end.

These thus in faire each other farre excelling,
As to the Highest they approch more neare,
Yet is that Highest farre beyond all telling,
Fairer then all the rest which there appeare,

Though all their beauties joind together were
How then can mortall tongue hope to expresse.
The image of such endlesse perfectnesse?

Cease then my tongue, and lend unto my mind
Leave to bethinke how great that beautie is,
Whose utmost parts so beautifull I find:
How much more those essentiall parts of his,
His truth, his love, his wisedome, and his blis,
His grace, his doome, his mercy and his might,
By which he lends us of himselfe a sight.

Those unto all he daily doth display,
And shew himselfe in th'image of his grace,
As in a looking glasse, through which he may
Be seene, of all his creatures vile and base,
That are unable else to see his face,
His glorious face which glistereth else so bright,
That th' Angels selves can not endure his sight.

But we fraile wights, whose sight cannot sustaine
The Suns bright beames, when he on us doth shine,
But that their points rebutted backe againe
Are duld, how can we see with feeble eyne,
The glory of that Majesty divine,
In sight of whom both Sun and Moone are darke,
Compared to his least resplendent sparke?

The meanes therefore which unto us is lent,
Him to behold, is on his workes to looke,
Which he hath made in beauty excellent,
And in the same, as in a brasen booke,
To reade enregistered in every nooke
His goodnesse, which his beautie doth declare.
For all that's good, is beautifull and faire.

Thence gathering plumes of perfect speculation,
To impe the wings of thy high flying mind,
Mount up aloft through heavenly contemplation,
From this darke world, whose damps the soule do blind,
And like the native brood of Eagles kind,
On that bright sunne of glorie fixe thine eyes,
Clear'd from grosse mists of fraile infirmities.

Humbled with feare and awfull reverence,
Before the footestoole of his Majesty,
Throw thy selfe downe with trembling innocence,
Ne dare looke up with corruptible eye
On the dred face of that great Deity,
For feare, lest is he chaunce to looke on thee,
Thou turne to nought, and quite confounded be.

But lowly fall before his mercie seate,
Close covered with the Lambes integrity,
From the just wrath of his avengefull threate,
That sits upon the righteous throne on hy:
His throne is built upon Eternity,
More firme and durable then stele or brasse,
Or the hard diamond, which them both doth passe.

His scepter is the rod of Righteousnesse,
With which he bruseth all his foes to dust,
And the great Dragon strongly doth represse,
Under the rigour of his judgement just;
His seate is Truth, to which the faithfull trust;
From whence proceed her beames so pure and bright,
That all about him sheddeth glorious light.

Light farre exceeding that bright blazing sparke,
Which darted is from Titans flaming head,
That with his beames enlumineth the darke
And dampish aire, whereby all things are red:
Whose nature yet so much is marvelled
Of mortall wits, that it doth much amaze
The greatest wisards, which thereon do gaze.

But that immortall light which there doth shine,
Is many thousand times more bright, more cleare,
More excellent, more glorious, more divine,
Through which to god all mortall actions here,
And even the thoughts of men, do plaine appeare
For from th' eternall Truth it doth proceed,
Through heavenly vertue, which her beames doe breed.

With the great glorie of that wondrous light,
His throne is all encompassed around,
And hid in his owne brightnesse from the sight

Of all that looke thereon with eyes unsound:
And underneath his feet are to be found
Thunder, and lightning, and tempestuous fire,
The instruments of his avenging ire.

There in his bosome Sapience doth sit,
The soveraine dearling of the Deity,
Clad like a Queene in royall robes, most fit
For so great powre and peerelesse majesty.
And all with gemmes and jewels gorgeously
Adornd that brighter then the starres appeare,
And make her native brightnes seem more cleare.

And on her head a crowne of purest gold
Is set, in signe of highest soveraignty,
And in her hand a scepter she doth hold,
With which she rules the house of God on hy,
And menageth the ever-moving sky,
And in the same these lower creatures all,
Subjected to her powre imperiall.

Both heaven and earth obey unto her will,
And all the creatures which they both containe:
For of her fulnesse which the world doth fill,
They all partake, and do in state remaine,
As their great maker did at first ordaine,
Through observation of her high beheast,
By which they first were made, and still creast.

The fairnesse of her face no tongue can tell,
For she the daughters of all wemens race,
And Angels eke, in beautie, doth excell,
Sparkled on her from Gods owne glorious face,
And more increast by her own goodly grace,
That it doth farre exceed all humane thought,
Ne can on earth compares be thought.

Ne could that Painter (had he lived yet)
Which pictured Venus with so curious quill,
That all posteritie admired it,
Have purtrayd this, for all his maistring skill;
Ne she her selfe, had she remaned still,
And were as faire, as fabling wits do fayne,
Could once come neare this beauty soverayne.

But had those wits the wonders of their dayes
Or that sweete Teian Poet which did spend
His plenteous vaine in setting forth her prayse,
Seene but a glims of thise, which I pretend,
How wondrously would he her face commend,
Above that Idole of his fayning thought,
That all the world shold with his rimes be fraught?

How then dare I, the novice of his Art,
Presume to picture so divine a wight,
Or hope t' expresse her least perfections part,
Whose beautie filles theheavens with her light,
And darkes the earth with shadow of her sight?
Ah gentle Muse thou art too weake and faint,
The pourtraict of so heavenly hew to paint.

Let Angels which her goodly face behold
And see at will, her soveraigne praises sing,
And those most sacred mysteries unfold,
Of that faire love of mightie heavens king.
Enough is me t' admire so heavenly thing,
And being thus with her huge love possest,
In th' only wonder of her selfe to rest.

But who so may, thise happie man him hold,
Of all on earth, whom God so much doth grace,
And lets his owne Beloved to behold:
For in the view of her celestiall face,
All joy, all blisse, all happinesse have place,
Ne ought on earth can want unto the wight,
Who of her selfe can win the wishfull sight.

For she out of her secret threasury,
Plentie of riches forth on him will powre,
Even heavenly riches, which here hidden ly
Within the closet of her chastest bowre,
Th' eternall portion of her precious dowre,
Which mighty God hath given to her free,
And to all those which thereof worthy bee.

None thereof worthy bee, but those whom she
Vouchsafeth to her presence to receave,
And letteth them her lovely face to see,

Whereof such wondrous pleasures they conceave,
And sweets contentment, that it doth bereave
Their soule of sense, through infinite delight,
And them transport from flesh into the spright.

In which they see such admirable things,
As carries them into an extasy,
And heare such heavenly notes, and carolings,
Of Gods high praise, that filles the brasen sky,
And feele such joy and pleasure inwardly,
That maketh them all wordly cares forget,
And onely thinke on that before them set.

Ne from thenceforth doth any fleshly sense,
Or idle thought of earthly things remaine:
But all that earst seemd sweet, seems now offense,
And all that pleased earst, now seemes to paine.
Their joy, their comfort, their desire, their gaine.
Is fixed all on that which now they see,
All other sights but fayned shadowes bee.

And that faire lampe, which useth to enflame
The hearts of men with self consuming fire,
Thenceforth seems fowle, and full of sinfull blame;
And all that pompe, to which proud minds aspire
By name of honor, and so much desire,
Seemes to them basenesse, and all riches drosse,
And all mirth sadnesse, and all lucre losse.

So full their eyes are of that glorious sight,
And senses fraught with such satietie,
That in nought else on earth they can delight,
But in th' aspect of that felicitie,
Which they have written in their inward eye;
On which they feed, and in their fastened mind
All happie joy and full contentment find.

Ah then my hungry soule, which long hast fed
On idle fancies of thy foolish thought,
And with false beauties flattring bait misled,
Hast after vaine deceiptfull shadowes sought,
Which all are fled, and now have left thee nought,
But late repentance through thy follies prief;
Ah ceasse to gaze on matter of thy grief.

And looke at last up to that soveraine light,
From whose pure beams all perfect beauty springs,
That kindeth love in every godly spright,
Even the love of God, which loathing brings
Of this vile world, and these gay seeming things;
With whose sweete pleasures being so possesst,
Thy straying thoughts henceforth for ever rest.

PROTHALAMION

1

Calme was the day, and through the trembling ayre,
Sweete breathing Zephyrus did softly play
A gentle sprit, that lightly did delay
Hot Titans beames, which then did glyster fayre:
When I whom sullein care,
Through discontent of my long fruitlesse stay
In Princes Court, and expectation vayne
Of idle hopes, which still doe fly away,
Like empty shaddowes, did afflict my brayne,
Walkt forth to ease my pane
Along the shoare of silver streaming Themes,
Whose rutty Bancke, the which his River hemmes,
Was paynted all with variable flowers,
And all the meades adornd with daintie gemmes,
Fit to decke maydens bowres,
And crowne their Paramours,
Against the Brydale day, which is not long:
       Sweete Themmes runne softly, till I end my song.

2

There, in a meadow, by the Rivers side,
A flocke of Nymphes I chaunced to espy,
All lovely Daughters of the Flood thereby,
With goodly greenish locks all loose untyde,
As each had bene a Bryde,
And each one had a little wicker basket,
Made of fine twigs entrayled curiously,
In which they gathered flowers to fill their flasket:
And with fine Fingers, cropt full feateously
The tender stalkes on hye.
Of every sort, which in that Meadow grew,
They gathered some; the Violet pallid blew,

The little Dazie, that at evening closes,
The virgin Lillie, and the Primrose trew,
With store of vermeil Roses,
To decke their Bridegromes posies,
Against the Brydale day, which was not long:
      Sweete Themmes runne softly, till I end my Song.

3

With that, I saw two Swannes of goodly hewe,
Come softly swimming downe along the Lee;
Two fairer Birds I yet did never see:
The snow which doth the top of Pindus strew,
Did never whiter shew,
Nor Jove himselfe when he a Swan would be
For love of Leda, whiter did appeare:
Yet Leda was they say as white as he,
Yet no white as these, nor nothing neare;
So purely white they were,
That even the gentle streame, the which them bare.
Seem'd foule to them, and bad his billowes spare
To wet their silken feathers, least they might
Soyle their fayre plumes with water not so fayre,
And marre their beauties bright,
That shone as heavens light,
Against their Brydale day, which was not long:
      Sweete Themmes runne softly, till I end my Song.

4

Eftsoones the Numphes, which now had Flowers their fill,
Ran all in haste, to see that silver brood,
As they came floating on the christal Flood.
Whom when they sawe, they stood amazed still,
Their wondering eyes to fill,
Them seem'd they never saw a sight so fayre,
Of Fowles so lovely, that they sure did deeme
Them heavenly borne, or to be that same payre,
Which through the Skie draw Venus silver Teeme,
For sure they did not seeme
To be begot of any earthly Seede,
But rather Angels or of Angels breede:

Yet were they bred of Sommers-heat they say,
In sweetest Season, when each Flower and weede
The earth did fresh aray,
So fresh they seem'd as day,
Even as their Byrdale day, which was not long:
       Sweete Themmes runne softly, till I end my Song.

5

The forth they all out of their baskets drew,
Great store of Flowers, the honour of the field,
That to the sense did fragrant odours yield,
All which upon those goodly Birds they threw,
And all the Ways did strew,
That like old Peneus Waters they did seeme,
Whend owne along by pleasant Tempes shore
Scattered with Flowers, through Thessaly they streeme,
That they appeare through lillies plenteous store,
Like a Brydes Chamber flore:
Two of those Nymphes, meane while, two Garlands bound,
Of freshest Flowers which in that mead they found,
The which presenting all in trim Array,
Their snowie Foreheads therewithall they crownd,
Whil'st one did sing this Lay,
Prepar'd against that Day,
Against their Brydale day, which was not long:
       Sweete Themmes runne softly, till I end my Song.

6

Ye gentle Birdes, the worlds faire ornament,
And heavens glorie, whom this happie hower
Doth leade unto your lovers blisfull bower,
Joy may you have and gentle hearts content
Of your loves complement:
And let faire Venus, that is Queene of love,
Withher heart-quelling Sonne upon you smile,
Whose smile they say, hath vertue to remove
All Loves dislike, and friendships faultie guile
For ever to assoile.
Let endlesse Peace your steadfast hearts accord,
And blessed Plentie wait upon your bord,

And let your bed with pleasures chast abound,
That fruitfull issue may to you afford,
Which may your foes confound,
And make your joyes redound,
Upon your Brydale day, which is not long:
      Sweete Themmes run softly, till I end my Song.

7

So ended she; and all the rest around
To her redoubled that her undersong,
Which said, their bridale daye should not be long,
And gentle Eccho from the neighbour ground,
Their accents did resound.
So forth those joyous Birdes did passe along,
Adowne the Lee, that to them murmurde low,
As he would speake, but that he lackt a tong
Yeat did by signes his glad affection show,
Making his streame run slow.
And all the foule which in his flood did dwell
Gan flock about these twaine, that did excell
The rest, so far, as Cynthia doth shend
The lesser starres. So they enranged well,
Did on those two attend,
And their best service lend,
Against their wedding day, which was not long:
      Sweete Themmes runne softly, till I end my Song.

8

At length they all to merry London came,
To merry London, my most kindly Nurse,
That to me gave this Lifes first native sourse:
Though from another place I take my name,
An house of aucient fame.
There when they came, whereas those bricky towres,
The which on Themes brode aged backe doe ride,
Where now the studious Lawyres have their bowers
There whilome wont the Templer Knights to bide,
Till they decayed through pride:
Next whereunto there standes a stately place,
Where oft I gained giftes and goodily grace

Of that great Lord, which therein wont to dwell,
Whose want too well now feeles my freendles case:
But Ah here fits not well
Olde woes but joyes to tell
Against the bridale daye, which is not long:
          Sweete Themmes runne softly, till I end my Song.

9

Yet therein now doth lodge a noble Peer,
Great Englands glory and the Worlds wide wonder,
Whose dreadfull name, late through all Spaine did thunder,
And Hercules two pillars standing neere,
Did make to quake and feare:
Faire branch of Honor, flower of Chevalrire,
That fillest England
With thy triumphs fame,
Joy have thou of thy noble victorie,
And endless happinese of thine owne name
That promiseth the same:
That through thy prowesse and victorious armes,
Thy country may be freed from forraine harmes:
And great Elisaes glorious name may ring
Through all the world, fil'd with thy wide Alarmes,
Which some brave muse may sing
To ages following,
Upon the Brydale day, which is not long,
          Sweete Themmes runne softly, till I end my Song.

Illustrations

Of Edmund Spenser, and art inspired by his works.

Edmund Spenser

Elizabeth I, anonymous artist, 1575,
National Portrait Gallery, London

William Etty, Britomart Redeems Faire Amoret, 1833, Tate Gallery

Briton Rivière, Una and the Lion, from The Fairie Queene

John Henry Fuseli, from The Faire Queene, 1788, Basel

John Hamilton Mortimer, Sir Arthegal, the Knight of Justice,
Faerie Queene, Tate Gallery

Florimell Saved By Proteus, by Walter Crane, 1895-97

Edmund Spenser's Faerie Queene, an edition from 1895

A Note On Edmund Spenser

by Teresa Page

Edmund Spenser created a drama of England in his poetry. The 'dream' occurs throughout his poetry, but finds its most concentrated expression in *The Faerie Queene*, with its epic treatment of the 'dream of Albion', a myth-making vision of Blighty as the expression of Elizabeth I's magnificence, and vice versa. *The Faerie Queene* is an astonishing work, by any standards, and it dwarfs, at times, even those other creations of the Renaissance that are so revered by readers and critics – Marlowe's *Doctor Faustus*, Shakespeare's plays and Sidney's *Astrophel and Stella*.

Elizabeth I appropriated the cult of the Virgin Mary, styling herself as the Virgin Queen of an Empire, according to Frances Yates:

The bejewelled and painted images of the Virgin Mary had been cast out of churches and monasteries, but another bejewelled and painted image was set up in court, and went in progress through the land for her worshippers to adore. The cult of the Virgin was regarded as one of the chief abuses of the unreformed Church, but it would be, perhaps, extravagant to suggest that, in a Christian country, the worship of the state Virgo was deliberately intended to take its place.[1]

This changeover from Catholic to Anglican allegiance is nothing new: many other monarchs and leaders have appropriated some mass feeling or politics for their own purposes. The power and influence of Elizabeth I and her 'nearly fifty years of myth-making', as Steve Davies puts it,[2] extended through the ages. It did not stop with her death; as Maureen Sabine explains how Elizabeth and her court rewrote Christianity, so the Queen of Heaven became the Queen of Britain:

Immediately upon her coronation, she took steps to suppress the belief that the mass was an offering of the true body of Christ which had really issued from the body of the Virgin Mary. In subsuming not only Corpus Christi but the fears of Mary to the propaganda of her provident rule, she made it clear that it was no longer Christ and his Mother but her body which constituted the immutable and vernal life of the church. her tenacious hold over English social life as reigning queen for nearly fifty years, her remarkable longevity and robustness of person and her immersion in the Marian role of ageless virgin-mother-spouse consecrated to her people helped to substantiate this monumental lie.[3]

There are many areas that are fascinating but too involved to deal with here: Edmund Spenser's relation to Queen Elizabeth, his use of the mythology of Elizabeth, the relation between his use of Classic mythology and contemporary British royal mythology, his use of pastoral imagery, the sociological and political picture presented in *The Faerie Queene*, the relation between Spenser and Shakespeare, between Spenser and courtly love poetry, between Spenser and Christianity, etc.[4]

The poem 'April', from *The Shepheardes Calendar*, in this book, is an extraordinary hymn to Elizabeth I, full of many poetic pleasures. It is an ecologue, as Simon Shepherd notes, that barely hides its sexism and patriarchal power relations:

The reader – who is assumed, crucially, to be male – is given a position of power which is constructed from the idea of viewing. A woman is decorated by a male text and looked at by a male readership as an object. The male poet's skill brings into being this decorated woman. The (male) reader consents to imagine and respond to the poet's vision. (32)

This occurs in most poetry: in Petrarch's *Canzoniere*, or Shakespeare's *Sonnets*, or Sidney's *Astrophel and Stella*, Keats' *Odes* or Goethe's lyrics the reader is assumed to be male. It happens in painting, where the subject is 'feminine' (the female nude, or the pastoral landscape, which is a Goddess, the Mother Earth). The subject is an object of pleasure, promising Arcadian delights. The viewer of 'high art' paintings is presumed to be male. It is a case of the male gaze controlling the female object of desire. Simon Shepherd continues:

Although pleasurable, this reader's position is clearly false. The hymn does not exhibit the language of Elizabethan myth, it employs its power... In brief, the hymn has been written by a poet whose 'mynd was alienate', and it is sung by his former but now rejected friend. While the text of the hymn celebrates fullness, its creator and performer are both frustrated and distressed. The glorification of Elisa/ Elizabeth need not presuppose the content of the glorifiers. (32-3)

In *The Faerie Queene* section included here, the frame is a mythical quest or journey. The pleasure is in following the hero on his quest, as in Arthurian legend. This is, again, a particularly masculine pleasure, as found in the masculinist pursuits of chivalry, hunting, courtly love, etc.

Technically, Edmund Spenser knew everything about poetry, it seems. He wrote many sonnets, and in his *The Faerie Queene* he wrote hundreds of nine-line stanzas. There is a stately progress to Spenser's poesie: he did not rush things. He took his time.

Wordsworth spoke of

> *Sweet Spenser, moving through his clouded heaven*
> *With the moon's beauty and the moon's soft pace*

In the *Amoretti*, Edmund Spenser tackled his target, his beloved, from many directions, as Michael Spiller notes in his excellent survey of the sonnet form:

> *Spenser, then, creates in the Amoretti an /I/ who desires one thing (marriage to his Lady) but performs his desire eloquently from various angels and in various voices and registers, within the range conventional to the sonnet discourse. So there is affectionate badinage (lxxi), erotic fantasia (lxxvi), anecdote (lxxv), self-reproach (lxxxiv), ironic conversation with others (xxix), extravagant addresses to Cupid (x) and moral commonplaces (xxvi); there are sonnets which address the Lady, others which talk about her, others which are private self-communings, even ones which have Sidney's (and Wyatt's) trick of suggesting a conversation in progress (xxxiii, lxv). There is also a variety of emotions directed towards the beloved: exasperation (x), adoration (viii), frustration (xxxvi), rage (lxvi), sexual desire (lxiv), companionship (lxxv), avuncular consolation (lxvi), loneliness (lxxxvii) and joy (lxxxii).*[5]

Edmund Spenser is unsurpassed in the art of poetic exaltation – no other poet of the era – and of subsequent or previous eras – attains Spenser's sense of the superlative, the exalted. Spenser's poetry is a litany of pæans: 'Epithalamion', 'A Hymn in Honour of Love', 'A Hymn in Honour of Beauty', 'A Hymn of Heavenly Beauty', 'A Hymn of Heavenly Love', 'Prothalamion', 'The Shepheardes Calendar' and of course *The Faerie Queene* all contain passages of lyrical praise. Like Shakespeare, Spenser's view of the world as crystallized in his poetry is an expansive, dramatic, encyclopaedic vision. The sheer amount of work by Spenser – the copious letters, 'Complaints', 'Hymns', sonnets, and stanzas in *The Faerie Queene* attest to his love of writing. The length of *The Faerie Queene* is not the least astonishing thing about it. Spenser clearly had a lot to say, and would not stop until he had said it. Works such as 'The Shepheardes Calendar' are also very long, while shorter pieces (for Spenser), such as the 'Epithalamion', are, by today's standards, lengthy works. This makes the entirety of Spenser's *œuvre* difficult to grasp, so all-encompassing is it, yet this is also partly why he is so central to English literature. Few other poets have written at such length and in such detail (one thinks of Shakespeare with his 37 or so plays, Dante and his *Divina Commedia*, and the long poem sequences of Milton, Shelley, Marlowe and Wordsworth). Length does not equal quality, but Spenser's range is so large, his learning so encyclopaedic (he recalls Sir Thomas Browne or John Dee in this respect) and his sense of occasion and detail so acute, his work remains, with Shakespeare, Chaucer, Wordsworth and Milton, absolutely the apotheosis of English poetry.

NOTES

1. Frances Yates, *Giordano Bruno and the Hermetic Tradition*, London 1964. See also Frances Yates: *The Rosicrucian Enlightenment*, Routledge 1972; Ted Hughes: *Shakespeare and the Goddess of Complete Being*, Faber 1992;D.P. Walker: *Spiritual and Demonic Magic from Ficino to Campanella*, Warburg Institute 1958; Wayne Shumaker: *The Occult Sciences in the Renaissance*, University of California Press, Berkeley, Calif., 1972; Walter Pagel: *Paracelsus: An Introduction to Philosophical Medicine in the Era of the Renaissance*, Karger, New York 1958; Peter French: *John Dee*, Routledge 1972

2. Stevie Davies: *The Idea of Woman in Renaissance Literature: The Feminine Reclaimed*, Harvester Press, Brighton 1986

3. Maureen Sabine: *Feminine Engendered Faith: The Poetry of John Donne and Richard Crashaw*, Macmillan 1992, 13

4. See, for starters: Louise Montrose: ""Eliza, Queene of Shepheardes" and the Pastoral of Power", in *English Language Review*, vol. X, 1980, 164-6; Elkin Calhoun Wilson: *England's Eliza*, Harvard Studies in English, vol. XX, Octagon, New York 1966; Robin Wells: *Spenser's Faerie Queene and the Cult of Elizabeth*, Barnes & Noble, Totowa, New Jersey 1983; Adrian Morey: *The Catholic Subjects of Elizabeth I*, Allen & Unwin 1978; William P. Haugaard: *Elizabeth and the English Reformation: The Struggle for a Stable Settlement of Religion*, Cambridge University Press, 1968; Margaret Ferguson *et al*, eds: *Rewriting the Renaissance: The Discourses of Sexual Difference in Early Modern Europe*, University of Chicago Press 1986; Carole Levin: "Power, politics, and sexuality: images of Elizabeth I", in Jean R. Brink *et al*, eds: *The Politics of Gender in Early Modern, Sixteenth Century Studies and Essays*, 12, 1989, 95-110; Leonard Tennenhouse: *Power on Display: The Politics of Shakespeare's Genres*, Methuen 1986; Roy Strong: *The Cult of Elizabeth I*, Thames & Hudson 1977

5. Michael R.G. Spiller: *The Development of the Sonnet: An Introduction*, Routledge 1992, 148

Life, Life
Selected Poems

Arseny Tarkovsky

translated and edited by Virginia Rounding

Arseny Tarkovsky is the neglected Russian poet, father of the acclaimed film director
Andrei Tarkovsky. This new book gathers together many of Tarkovsky's most lyrical
and heartfelt poems, in Rounding's clear, new translations. Many of Tarkovsky's poems
appeared in his son's films, such as *Mirror, Stalker, Nostalghia and The Sacrifice*.
There is an introduction by Rounding, and a bibliography of both Arseny and
Andrei Tarkovsky.

Bibliography and notes 124pp 3rd ed   ISBN 9781861712660 Hbk ISBN 9781861711144

In the Dim Void

Samuel Beckett's Late Trilogy:
Company, Ill Seen, Ill Said and *Worstward Ho*

by Gregory Johns

This book discusses the luminous beauty and dense, rigorous poetry of Samuel Beckett's late works, *Company, Ill Seen, Ill Said* and *Worstward Ho*. Gregory Johns looks back over Beckett's long writing career, charting the development from the *Molloy-Malone Dies-Unnamable* trilogy through the 'fizzles' of the 1960s to the elegiac lyricism of the *Company* series. Johns compares the trilogy with late plays such as *Ghosts, Footfalls* and *Rockaby*.

Bibliography, notes. Illustrated. 120pp
ISBN 9781861712974 Pbk and ISBN 9781861712608 Hbk
9781861713407 E-book

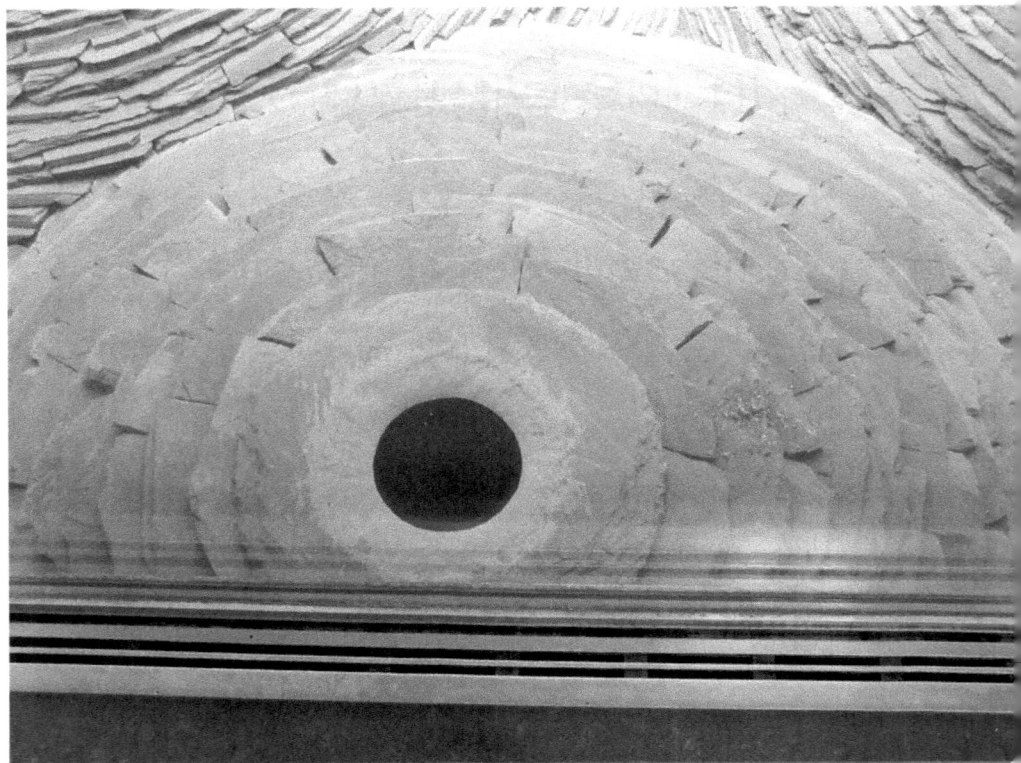

andy goldsworthy
touching nature

WILLIAM MALPAS

Contemporary British sculptor Andy Goldsworthy makes land and
environmental art, a sensitive, intuitive response to nature, light, time,
growth, change, the seasons and the earth. Goldsworthy's sculpture is
becoming ever more popular, appearing in TV documentaries, public works,
and Holocaust memorials. Goldsworthy has exhibited around the world, and
has become one of the foremost contemporary sculptors in Great Britain.

The book has been updated and revised for this new edition.

ISBN 9781861714122 Pbk   ISBN 9781861714138 Hbk
Fully illustrated   www.crmoon.com

Beauties, Beasts, and Enchantment

CLASSIC FRENCH FAIRY TALES

Translated and with an Introduction
by Jack Zipes

A collection of 36 classic French fairy tales translated by renowned writer Jack Zipes.
Cinderella, Beauty and the Beast, Sleeping Beauty and *Little Red Riding Hood* are among the
classic fairy tales in this amazing book.
Includes illustrations from fairy tale collections.
Jack Zipes has written and published widely on fairy tales.

'Terrific... a succulent array of 17th and 18th century 'salon' fairy tales'
- *The New York Times Book Review*

'These tales are adventurous, thrilling in a way fairy tales are meant to be... The translation
from the French is modern, happily free of archaic and hyperbolic language... a fine and
sophisticated collection' - *New York Tribune*

'Enjoyable to read... a unique collection of French regional folklore' - *Library Journal*

'Charming stories accompanied by attractive pen-and-ink drawings' - *Chattanooga Times*

Introduction and illustrations   612pp.   ISBN 9781861712510 Pbk   ISBN 9781861713193 Hbk

CRESCENT MOON PUBLISHING

web: www.crmoon.com e-mail: cresmopub@yahoo.co.uk

ARTS, PAINTING, SCULPTURE

The Art of Andy Goldsworthy
Andy Goldsworthy: Touching Nature
Andy Goldsworthy in Close-Up
Andy Goldsworthy: Pocket Guide
Andy Goldsworthy In America
Land Art: A Complete Guide
The Art of Richard Long
Richard Long: Pocket Guide
Land Art In the UK
Land Art in Close-Up
Land Art In the U.S.A.
Land Art: Pocket Guide
Installation Art in Close-Up
Minimal Art and Artists In the 1960s and After
Colourfield Painting
Land Art DVD, TV documentary
Andy Goldsworthy DVD, TV documentary
The Erotic Object: Sexuality in Sculpture From Prehistory to the Present Day
Sex in Art: Pornography and Pleasure in Painting and Sculpture
Postwar Art
Sacred Gardens: The Garden in Myth, Religion and Art
Glorification: Religious Abstraction in Renaissance and 20th Century Art
Early Netherlandish Painting
Leonardo da Vinci
Piero della Francesca
Giovanni Bellini
Fra Angelico: Art and Religion in the Renaissance
Mark Rothko: The Art of Transcendence
Frank Stella: American Abstract Artist
Jasper Johns
Brice Marden
Alison Wilding: The Embrace of Sculpture
Vincent van Gogh: Visionary Landscapes
Eric Gill: Nuptials of God
Constantin Brancusi: Sculpting the Essence of Things
Max Beckmann
Caravaggio
Gustave Moreau
Egon Schiele: Sex and Death In Purple Stockings
Delizioso Fotografico Fervore: Works In Process 1
Sacro Cuore: Works In Process 2
The Light Eternal: J.M.W. Turner
The Madonna Glorified: Karen Arthurs

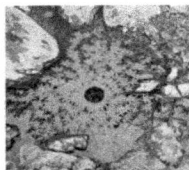

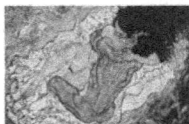

LITERATURE

J.R.R. Tolkien: The Books, The Films, The Whole Cultural Phenomenon
J.R.R. Tolkien: Pocket Guide
Tolkien's Heroic Quest
The *Earthsea* Books of Ursula Le Guin
Beauties, Beasts and Enchantment: Classic French Fairy Tales
German Popular Stories by the Brothers Grimm
Philip Pullman and *His Dark Materials*
Sexing Hardy: Thomas Hardy and Feminism
Thomas Hardy's *Tess of the d'Urbervilles*

Thomas Hardy's *Jude the Obscure*
Thomas Hardy: The Tragic Novels
Love and Tragedy: Thomas Hardy
The Poetry of Landscape in Hardy
Wessex Revisited: Thomas Hardy and John Cowper Powys
Wolfgang Iser: Essays and Interviews
Petrarch, Dante and the Troubadours
Maurice Sendak and the Art of Children's Book Illustration
Andrea Dworkin

Cixous, Irigaray, Kristeva: The *Jouissance* of French Feminism
Julia Kristeva: Art, Love, Melancholy, Philosophy, Semiotics and Psychoanalysis
Hélene Cixous I Love You: The *Jouissance* of Writing
Luce Irigaray: Lips, Kissing, and the Politics of Sexual Difference
Peter Redgrove: Here Comes the Flood
Peter Redgrove: Sex-Magic-Poetry-Cornwall
Lawrence Durrell: Between Love and Death, East and West
Love, Culture & Poetry: Lawrence Durrell

Cavafy: Anatomy of a Soul
German Romantic Poetry: Goethe, Novalis, Heine, Hölderlin
Feminism and Shakespeare
Shakespeare: Love, Poetry & Magic
The Passion of D.H. Lawrence

D.H. Lawrence: Symbolic Landscapes
D.H. Lawrence: Infinite Sensual Violence
Rimbaud: Arthur Rimbaud and the Magic of Poetry
The Ecstasies of John Cowper Powys
Sensualism and Mythology: The Wessex Novels of John Cowper Powys
Amorous Life: John Cowper Powys and the Manifestation of Affectivity (H.W. Fawkner)
Postmodern Powys: New Essays on John Cowper Powys (Joe Boulter)
Rethinking Powys: Critical Essays on John Cowper Powys
Paul Bowles & Bernardo Bertolucci
Rainer Maria Rilke
Joseph Conrad: *Heart of Darkness*
In the Dim Void: Samuel Beckett

Samuel Beckett Goes into the Silence
André Gide: Fiction and Fervour
Jackie Collins and the Blockbuster Novel
Blinded By Her Light: The Love-Poetry of Robert Graves
The Passion of Colours: Travels In Mediterranean Lands
Poetic Forms

POETRY

Ursula Le Guin: Walking In Cornwall
Peter Redgrove: Here Comes The Flood
Peter Redgrove: Sex-Magic-Poetry-Cornwall
Dante: Selections From the Vita Nuova
Petrarch, Dante and the Troubadours
William Shakespeare: Sonnets
William Shakespeare: Complete Poems
Blinded By Her Light: The Love-Poetry of Robert Graves
Emily Dickinson: Selected Poems
Emily Brontë: Poems
Thomas Hardy: Selected Poems
Percy Bysshe Shelley: Poems
John Keats: Selected Poems
Joh n Keats: Poems of 1820
D.H. Lawrence: Selected Poems
Edmund Spenser: Poems
Edmund Spenser: Amoretti
John Donne: Poems
Henry Vaughan: Poems
Sir Thomas Wyatt: Poems
Robert Herrick: Selected Poems
Rilke: Space, Essence and Angels in the Poetry of Rainer Maria Rilke
Rainer Maria Rilke: Selected Poems
Friedrich Hölderlin: Selected Poems
Arseny Tarkovsky: Selected Poems
Arthur Rimbaud: Selected Poems
Arthur Rimbaud: A Season in Hell
Arthur Rimbaud and the Magic of Poetry
Novalis: Hymns To the Night
German Romantic Poetry
Paul Verlaine: Selected Poems
Elizaethan Sonnet Cycles
D.J. Enright: By-Blows
Jeremy Reed: Brigitte's Blue Heart
Jeremy Reed: Claudia Schiffer's Red Shoes
Gorgeous Little Orpheus
Radiance: New Poems
Crescent Moon Book of Nature Poetry
Crescent Moon Book of Love Poetry
Crescent Moon Book of Mystical Poetry
Crescent Moon Book of Elizabethan Love Poetry
Crescent Moon Book of Metaphysical Poetry
Crescent Moon Book of Romantic Poetry
Pagan America: New American Poetry

MEDIA, CINEMA, FEMINISM and CULTURAL STUDIES

J.R.R. Tolkien: The Books, The Films, The Whole Cultural Phenomenon
J.R.R. Tolkien: Pocket Guide
The *Lord of the Rings* Movies: Pocket Guide
The Cinema of Hayao Miyazaki
Hayao Miyazaki: *Princess Mononoke*: Pocket Movie Guide
Hayao Miyazaki: *Spirited Away*: Pocket Movie Guide
Tim Burton : Hallowe'en For Hollywood
Ken Russell
Ken Russell: *Tommy*: Pocket Movie Guide
The Ghost Dance: The Origins of Religion
The Peyote Cult
Cixous, Irigaray, Kristeva: The *Jouissance* of French Feminism
Julia Kristeva: Art, Love, Melancholy, Philosophy, Semiotics and Psychoanalysis
Luce Irigaray: Lips, Kissing, and the Politics of Sexual Difference
Hélene Cixous I Love You: The *Jouissance* of Writing
Andrea Dworkin
'Cosmo Woman': The World of Women's Magazines
Women in Pop Music
HomeGround: The Kate Bush Anthology
Discovering the Goddess (Geoffrey Ashe)
The Poetry of Cinema
The Sacred Cinema of Andrei Tarkovsky
Andrei Tarkovsky: Pocket Guide
Andrei Tarkovsky: *Mirror*: Pocket Movie Guide
Andrei Tarkovsky: *The Sacrifice*: Pocket Movie Guide
Walerian Borowczyk: Cinema of Erotic Dreams
Jean-Luc Godard: The Passion of Cinema
Jean-Luc Godard: *Hail Mary*: Pocket Movie Guide
Jean-Luc Godard: *Contempt*: Pocket Movie Guide
Jean-Luc Godard: *Pierrot le Fou*: Pocket Movie Guide
John Hughes and Eighties Cinema
Ferris Bueller's Day Off: Pocket Movie Guide
Jean-Luc Godard: Pocket Guide
The Cinema of Richard Linklater
Liv Tyler: Star In Ascendance
Blade Runner and the Films of Philip K. Dick
Paul Bowles and Bernardo Bertolucci
Media Hell: Radio, TV and the Press
An Open Letter to the BBC
Detonation Britain: Nuclear War in the UK
Feminism and Shakespeare
Wild Zones: Pornography, Art and Feminism
Sex in Art: Pornography and Pleasure in Painting and Sculpture
Sexing Hardy: Thomas Hardy and Feminism

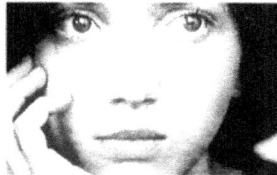

The Light Eternal is a model monograph, an exemplary job. The subject matter of the book is beautifully
organised and dead on beam. (Lawrence Durrell)
It is amazing for me to see my work treated with such passion and respect. (Andrea Dworkin)

CRESCENT MOON PUBLISHING
P.O. Box 1312, Maidstone, Kent, ME14 5XU, Great Britain. www.crmoon.com

cresmopub@yahoo.co.uk   www.crescentmoon.org.uk